AUTHENTIC
WINE SOUSED
RECIPES

100 EFFORTLESS
RECIPES

HENRI FLAMINI

Sommario

INTRODUCTION

Infusing with wine can be a pleasure and an enhancement to good food, drink and a fine meal! When wine is heated, the alcoholic content as well as sulfites disappears, leaving only the essence imparting a subtle flavor.

The first and most important rule: Use only wines in your cooking or drinks that you would drink. Never use any wine that you WOULD NOT DRINK! If you do not like the taste of a wine, you will not like the dish and drink you choose to use it in.

Do not use the so-called "cooking wines!" These wine are typically salty and include other additives that my affect the taste of your chosen dish and menu. The process of cooking/reducing will bring out the worst in an inferior wine.

Wine has three main uses in the kitchen - as a marinade ingredient, as a cooking liquid, and as a flavoring in a finished dish.

The function of wine in cooking is to intensify, enhance, and accent the flavor and aroma of food - not to mask the flavor of what you are cooking but rather to fortify it.

For best results, wine should not be added to a dish just before serving. The wine should simmer with the food, or sauce, to enhance the flavour. It should simmer with the food or in the sauce while it is being cooked; as the wine cooks, it reduces and becomes an extract which flavors.

Remember that wine does not belong in every dish. More than one wine based sauce in a single meal can be monotonous. Use wine is cooking only when it has something to contribute to the finished dish.

INFUSED WINES

1. White Sangria Infused Wine

Ingredients

- 1/2 lime
- 1/2 lemon
- 1 peach
- 1/2 green apple
- 1.5 cups wine

Directions:

a) Make sure the wine is at least room temperature or slightly warmer.

b) Lightly scrub the outside of the lime and lemon then remove the zest with a vegetable peeler or zester. Make sure little to no pith came off as well, using a paring knife to remove any. Lightly scrub the outside of the apple then core it and coarsely dice it. Lightly scrub the outside of the peach then remove the pit and coarsely dice the flesh.

c) Place all of the ingredients into the whipping siphon with the wine. Seal the whipping siphon, charge it, and swirl for 20 to 30 seconds. Let the siphon sit for a minute and a half longer. Place a towel over the top of the siphon and vent it. Open the siphon and wait until the bubbling stops.

d) Strain the wine if desired and let sit for at least 5 minutes before using.

2. Oranges and figs in spiced red wine

Ingredient

- 2 cups Red wine

- 1 cup Sugar

- 1 Piece Cinnamon stick

- 4 Star anise; tied together with

- 4 Cardamom pods; tied together with

15

- 2 Whole cloves

- 6 larges Navel oranges; peeled

- 12 Dried figs; halved

- ⅓cup Walnuts or pistachios; chopped

a) Combine the wine, sugar and bouquet garni in a saucepan large enough to contain the oranges and figs in a single layer. Bring to a simmer, covered, over moderate heat.

b) Add the figs and simmer for 5 minutes. Add the oranges and turn them for 3 to 4 minutes, turning them so they cook evenly.

c) Turn the heat off and let the oranges and figs cool in the syrup. Remove fruit to a serving bowl. Reduce the syrup by half and let cool. Discard bouquet garnish and spoon syrup over figs and oranges.

3. Star Anise Coffee Infused Wine

Ingredients

For the coffee-infused red wine

- 5 tablespoons roast coffee beans
- 1 750 mL bottle dry Italian red wine
- 1 cup water
- 1 cup turbinado sugar
- 12 star anise

For the cocktail

- 3 ounces coffee-infused red wine

- 1 ounce Cocchi Vermouth di Torino, chilled
- 2 teaspoons star anise syrup
- 2 dashes Fee Brothers Aztec bitters
- Ice (optional)
- Garnish: cinnamon stick or lemon curl

Directions

a) For the coffee-infused red wine: Add coffee beans to bottle of wine, close with stopper and infuse at room temperature for 24 hours. Strain before using.

b) For the star anise syrup: Bring water, sugar, and star anise to a boil, stirring until sugar dissolves. Remove from heat and let infuse for 30 minutes. Strain and bottle, keep refrigerated.

c) For each drink: in a wine glass, stir coffee-infused wine, Cocchi vermouth, star anise syrup, and chocolate bitters. Add ice if desired and garnish.

4. Rose, strawberry and grape wine

INGREDIENTS

- 100g strawberries, hulled and sliced
- 1 medium red grapefruit, sliced into rounds
- 1 rosehip sprig, optional (if in season)
- 1 tsp rose water
- 700ml rosé blush wine

Directions:

a) Put the strawberries, sliced grapefruit and rose water in a sterilised one-litre glass jar or bottle and pour over the rosé. Seal the jar tightly and store in the refrigerator overnight, gently shaking the jar occasionally to help infuse the flavours.

b) When you're ready to serve, strain the rosé through a fine-mesh sieve lined with muslin or a clean J cloth into a large jug, and discard the fruit.

c) To serve, add sparkling water to one quantity rose, strawberry and red grapefruit wine, and garnish with rose petals. For a rose Aperol spritz, mix 200ml infused rosé with 25ml Aperol and garnish with a slice of grapefruit.

5. Ice Wine Peaches

INGREDIENTS

- 6 fresh peaches, skinned, pitted and halved
- ½ cup sugar (125 ml)
- 1 cup ice wine (250 ml)
- 1 cup of water (250 ml)

DIRECTIONS

a) In a sauce pan combine 1 cup of water, sugar and ice wine and simmer over low heat and until the sugar has dissolved. Cook syrup for 3 additional minutes, take off the heat and set aside until needed.

b) In a glass bowl, place peach halves and pour ice wine syrup on top and refrigerate to allow the flavors to mix.

c) Serve chilled in a small bowl and garnish with a drizzle of icing sugar.

6. Lemon and Rosemary Wine

Ingredients

- 1 bottle white wine I would use Sauvignon Blanc, Pinot Gris, Pinot Grigio or Riesling
- 4 sprigs fresh rosemary
- 3-4 long pieces of lemon peel trying not to get the white pith on it

Directions:

a) Open your bottle of wine or use that bottle that's been in your fridge for a few days.

b) Clean and dry your herbs (in this case rosemary).

c) With a vegetable peeler, remove 4-5 long pieces of lemon zest taking care not to get too much of the white pitch.

d) Add rosemary and lemon zest to the wine bottle.

e) Add a cork and put it in your fridge overnight to several days.

f) Discard the lemon peel and herbs.

g) Drink the wine.

7. Homemade kiwi wine

Ingredient

- 75 Ripe kiwi

- 2 pounds Red grapes, frozen

- 12 ounces   100% grape concentrate

- 10 pounds   Sugar

- 2 packs Yeast

a) peel kiwi, mash with thawed grapes, put sugar
   into carboy, dissolve completly, add mashed

fruit, grape concentrate, water (appx 4 gallons) and yeast.

b) Ferment as usual. this is just the first racking taste

8. Mangoes in wine (tahiti)

Ingredient

- 12 Ripe mangoes

- ⅔litre   Red wine

- 130 grams   Castor sugar

- 2 Pods fresh vanilla

a) Remove skin from the mangoes and slice in two, removing the seeds.

b) Arrange with hollow side upwards in a large bowl and cover with wine.

c) Add sugar and vanilla pods. Bake for 45 minutes, allow cooling and then chilling well before serving.

9. Dandelion wine

Ingredient

- 4 quarts Dandelion blossoms

- 4 quarts Boiling water

- 6 Oranges

- 4 Lemons

- 2 Yeast cakes

- 4 pounds Sugar

a) Scald the blossoms in the boiling water and let stand overnight. The next morning, strain, add the pulp and juice of 6 oranges, the juice of 4 lemons, the yeast and the sugar. Let ferment for 4 days, then strain and bottle. Serve in small glasses at room temperature.

10. Hot apple wine

Ingredient

- ½ cup   Raisins

- 1 cup   Light rum

- 6 cups   Apple wine or hard cider

- 2 cups   Orange juice

- ⅓cup   Brown sugar

- 6 Whole cloves

- 2 Cinnamon sticks

- 1 Orange, slice

a) In small bowl, soak raisins in rum for several hours or overnight.

b) In large saucepan, combine all ingredients and heat, stirring often, until sugar dissolves. Simmer gently until hot. Do not boil. Serve in heatproof punch cups or mugs. Makes 9 cups

11. Fireside hot cranberry wine cup

Ingredient

- 4.00 cup Cranberry juice cocktail

- 2.00 cup Water

- 1.00 cup Sugar

- 4.00 Inches stick cinnamon

- 12.00 Cloves, whole

- 1.00 Peel of 1/2 lemon, cut in

- 1.00 Strips

- 2.00 Fifth of dry wine

- $\frac{1}{4}$ cup Lemon juice

a) Combine cranberry juice, water, sugar, cinnamon, cloves, and lemon peel in sauce pan. Bring to a boil, stirring until sugar is disolved.

b) Simmer, uncovered, 15 minutes, strain. Add wine and lemon juice, heat thoroughly, but DO NOT BOIL. Sprinkle nutmeg atop each serving, if desired.

12. Pepper wine

Ingredient

- 6 Pepper, red, hot; fresh

- 1 pint Rum, light

a) Put the whole peppers into a glass jar and pour in the rum (or dry sherry). Cover tightly with the lid and allow standing 10 days before using.

b) Use a few drops in soups or sauce. Pepper vinegar is made in the same way.

c) If fresh peppers are not available, whole, hot dried peppers may be used.

13. Pineapple in port wine

Ingredient

- 1 mediumPineapple, cleaned (about 2-1/2 lbs)

- Finely pared zest of 1 orange

- Finely pared zest of 1/2 grapefruit

- 4 tablespoons   Light brown sugar, or to taste

- $\frac{3}{4}$ cup   Pineapple juice

- $\frac{1}{2}$ cup   Port

a) This is a particularly good treatment for a
   pineapple that turns out not to be as sweet as

it should be. The better the port, the better the dessert. Make this dessert a day ahead for the best flavour.

b) Peel, slice and core the pineapple and cut into 1 inch cubes or thin slices. In pan, cook the zests, sugar and pineapple juice. Cook until the zests are tender, about 5 minutes. While the liquid is still warm, add the pineapple pieces and stir in the port.

c) Refrigerate for at least 8 hours, or overnight. Allow to come up to room temperature before serving or flavors will be lost.

14. Rhubarb wine

Ingredient

- 3 pounds Rhubarb

- 3 pounds White sugar

- 1 teaspoon   Yeast nutrient

- 1 gallon   Hot water (doesn't have to be boiling)

- 2 Campden tablets (crushed)

- Wine yeast

a) Chop up your rhubarb stalks and freeze them
   in plastic bags for a few days before you make

the wine. I really don't understand why this should make a difference, but it does. If you use fresh rhubarb the wine never comes out as good.

b) You have to have patience. Rhubarb wine can taste uninteresting at eight months and really good at ten months. You have to let it mellow.

c) Use frozen cut up rhubarb. Put it in the primary fermentor along with the sugar. Cover and let stand for 24 hours. Add the hot water, mix everything together and then strain out the rhubarb .

d) Put the liquid back in the primary fermentor and when it is luke-warm add the rest of the ingredients.

e) Cover and leave it to ferment for three or four days. Then syphon the liquid into gallon jugs with fermentation locks.

15. Gluehwein (hot spiced wine)

Ingredient

- ¼ litre   White or red wine (1 cup plus 1 Tbsp)
  6 sugar cubes, or to taste

- 1 each   Whole clove

- 1 small   Piece lemon peel

- A little stick cinnamon

Combine all ingredients and heat, barely to boiling point. Pour into a pre-warmed glass, wrap glass in a napkin, and serve immediately.

16. Cranberry-Infused Wine

Ingredient

- 2 c. dry white wine, such as Sauvignon Blanc or Chardonnay
- 1 c. fresh or frozen thawed cranberries

Directions

a) Add wine and cranberries to a container with a tight-fitting lid.

b) Cover and shake a few times. Let stand at room temperature overnight. Strain before using; discard cranberries.

17. Raspberry Mint Infused Wine

Ingredients

- 1 cup fresh raspberries
- 1 small bunch fresh mint
- 1 bottle white wine dry or sweet, whatever your preference

Directions:

a) Put the raspberries and mint in a quart sized jar. Use a spoon to crush the raspberries up slightly.

b) Pour the entire bottle of wine over the raspberries and mint, then cover with a lid and put in a quiet spot in your kitchen.

c) Let the infusion steep for 2-3 days, then strain out the raspberries and mint with a fine mesh sieve and enjoy!

18. Love-Infused Wine

Ingredients

- 1 glass jar 1 litre or 1 quart size
- 2 tsp cinnamon powder or 2 cinnamon sticks
- 3 tsp ginger root powder or fresh ginger root peeled about 1 inch long
- option 1 -- 1 inch piece of vanilla bean or 1 tsp vanilla extract
- or option 2 -- 2 cardamom pods + 2 star anise

- 3 cups red wine or one 750 ml bottle

Directions:

a) Add the red wine to the jar

b) Add the herbal components

c) Stir to mix ingredients.

d) Place lid on the jar. Put into a cool, dark cupboard for 3-5 days.

e) Strain well (or 2x) into another jar or a pretty glass decanter. It's ready!!!

19. Apples in red wine

Ingredient

- 1 kilograms   Apples (2 1/4 lb) You NEED an
  apple that will hold its shape during cooking !!

- 5 decilitres   Red wine (1 pint)

- 1 Stick cinnamon

- 250 grams   Sugar (9 oz)

a) Ten hours in advance, cook the wine, cinnamon and sugar over a brisk heat for 10 minutes, using a broad, shallow saucepan.

b) Peel the apples and, using a melon-baller of about $2\frac{1}{2}$ cm (1 in) diameter, cut them into little balls.

c) Throw the apple-balls into the hot wine. They should not overlap: this is why you need a broad, shallow pan. Simmer them for 5 to 7 minutes, covered with aluminium foil to keep them submerged.

d) When the apples are cooked but still firm, remove the pan from the stove. Let the apple-balls macerate in the red wine for about 10 hours to take on a good red colour.

e) Serving: well chilled, with a scoop of vanilla ice-cream, or in a selection of cold fruit desserts.

20. Bajan pepper wine

Ingredient

- 18 "wine peppers" or similar quantity of the tiny red peppers

- Barbados white rum

- Sherry

a) Remove stems from the peppers and place in a bottle, then cover with rum and leave for two weeks.

b) Strain and dilute to required "hotness" with sherry.

21. Orange dessert wine

Ingredient

- 5 eaches Oranges, Louisiana Naval

- 2 eaches Lemons

- 5 quarts Wine, dry white

- 2 pounds Sugar

- 4 cups   Brandy

- 1 each   Vanilla bean

- 1 each   Piece (1/2) orange rind, dry

a) Grate the skins of the oranges and lemons and reserve. Quarter the fruit and place in a demi-john or other large container (crock or glass).

b) Pour in the wine, then add the grated skins, sugar, brandy, vanilla bean and piece of dried orange rind.

c) Close off the jar and store in a cool dark place for 40 days. Strain through cloth and bottle. Serve chilled.

22. Orange with red wine syrup

Ingredient

- 2 cups Full-flavored red wine

- ½ cup Sugar

- 1 3" piece cinnamon stick

- 2 mediums Orange-fleshed honeydew melons or cantaloupes

a) In a medium nonreactive saucepan, combine the wine, sugar and cinnamon. Bring to a boil over high heat and cook until reduced by half, about 12 minutes.

b) Remove the cinnamon and let the syrup cool to room temperature

c) Halve the melons crosswise and discard the seeds. Cut a thin slice from the bottom of each melon half so that it sits upright and set each half on a plate.

d) Pour the red wine syrup into the melon halves and serve with large spoons.

23. Orange wine (vin d'orange)

Ingredient

- 3 Naval oranges; halved

- 1 cup   Sugar

- 1 quart   White wine

- 2 mediums   Naval oranges

- 20 Whole cloves

a) In a saucepan, over medium heat, squeeze the orange halves into the saucepan, add the squeezed oranges and the sugar. Bring to a boil, reduce the heat to low and simmer for 5 minutes. Remove from the heat and cool completely.

b) Strain into a $1\frac{1}{2}$ quart jar, pressing the oranges with the back of a spoon to release all of the juice. Stir in the wine. Stick the cloves into the whole oranges. Cut the oranges in half and add to the jar.

c) Secure the lid tightly and allow to sit for at least 24 hours and up to 1 month.

24. Ginger wine

Ingredient

- $\frac{1}{4}$ pounds Ginger
- 4 pounds D.C. sugar
- 1 gallon Water
- 2 teaspoons Yeast
- $\frac{1}{2}$ pounds Dried fruit
- $\frac{1}{2}$ ounce Mace

a) Crush ginger and put into a jar. Add all other ingredients and leave for 21 days.

b) Strain and bottle.

25. Mulled Wine

Tools You Need.

- Citrus juicer
- Wine bottle opener
- Sharp knife
- Large pot
- Strainer
- Mugs

Ingredients

- 1 Bottle red wine
- 2 Oranges

- 3 Cinnamon sticks
- 5 Star anise
- 10 Whole cloves
- 3/4 cup Brown sugar

Directions:

a) Place all ingredients except the oranges into a medium sized pot.

b) Using a sharp knife or peeler, peel half of one orange. Avoid peeling as much pith (white part) as possible, as it has a bitter taste.

c) Juice the oranges and add to the pot along with the orange peel.

d) Over medium heat, warm the mixture until just steaming. Reduce the heat to a low simmer. Heat for 30 minutes to let the spices infuse.

e) Strain the wine and serve into heat-proof cups.

26. Wine cooler

Ingredient

- 1.00   Serving

- ¾ cup   Lemonade

- ¼ cup   Dry red wine

- Sprig of mint

- Maraschino cherry

a) This makes a colorful as well as refreshing drink if the liquids are not mixed together. Pour the lemonade over crushed ice, then add the red wine.

b) Garnish with a sprig of mint and a cherry. Good for hot days.

27. Wine eggnog

Yield: 20 Servings

Ingredient

- 4.00 Egg whites

- 1 Fifth dry white wine

- ½ cup Fresh lemon juice

- 1.00 tablespoonLemon rind; grated

- 1.00 cup Honey

- 6.00 cup Milk

- 1.00 quart Half-and-half

- 1.00 Nutmeg; freshly grated

a) Beat egg whites until stiff and set aside. Combine wine, lemon juice, zest and honey in a large saucepan. Heat, stirring, until warm, then slowly add milk and cream.

b) Continue to heat and stir until mixture is frothy; remove from heat. Fold in egg whites and serve in mugs with a sprinkling of nutmeg on top.

28. Peach wine cooler

Ingredient

- 16 ounces   Unsweetened peaches; thawed

- 1 quart   Peach juice

- 750 millilitres Dry white wine; = 1 bottle

- 12 ounces   Apricot nectar

- 1 cup   Sugar

a) In a blender or food processor puree peaches. In a container, combine peaches and remaining ingredients.

b) Cover and chill 8 hours or overnight to allow flavors to blend. Store in refrigerator. Serve chilled.

INFUSED DESSERTS

29. Fruit and wine compote

Ingredient

- 4 smalls Pears

- 1 Orange

- 12 Moist prunes

- A 2.5 cm; (1 in) stick; cinnamon

- 2 Coriander seeds

- 1 Clove

- $\frac{1}{4}$ Bay leaf; (optional)

- ⅓ Vanilla pod

- 4 tablespoons Castor sugar

- $1\frac{1}{2}$ cup Good red wine

a) Peel pears, and wash and cut orange into $\frac{1}{2}$ cm ($\frac{1}{4}$ in) slices.

b) Gently place pears, stalk up, in saucepan. Place prunes in between pears and add cinnamon, coriander seeds, clove, bay leaf, vanilla and castor sugar.

c) Top with orange slices and add wine. If necessary add water so that there is just enough liquid to cover the fruit.

d) Bring to boil, lower to a simmer, and poach pears for 25 to 30 minutes until soft. Leave fruit to cool in liquid.

e) Remove spices and serve fruit and liquid from an attractive serving dish.

30. Chocolate Truffles

Ingredients

- 1 10-oz bag semi-sweet chocolate chips
- 1/2 cup heavy whipping cream
- 1 tablespoon unsalted butter
- 2 tablespoons red wine
- 1 teaspoon vanilla extract
- Toppings: crushed smoked almonds, cocoa powder, melted chocolate and sea salt

Directions:

a) Chop up the chocolate: Whether you're using a block of chocolate or chocolate chips, you're going to want to chop them up to make them melt easier. See notes for troubleshooting. Place the chopped chocolate in a large stainless steel or glass bowl.

b) Heat up Cream and Butter: Heat the cream and butter in a small saucepan over medium heat, just until it starts to boil.

c) Combine Cream with Chocolate: As soon as the liquid starts to boil immediately pour it into the bowl over the chocolate.

d) Add Additional Liquids: Add the vanilla and wine and whisk until smooth.

e) Refrigerate/Cool: Cover the bowl with plastic wrap and transfer to the refrigerator for about an hour (or in the freezer for 30 mins-1 hour), until the mixture is firm.

f) Roll Truffles: Once the truffles have cooled, scoop them out using a melon baller and roll them with your hands. This will get messy!

g) Then coat them with your desired toppings. I love crushed smoked almonds, cocoa powder, and melted tempered chocolate with sea salt.

31. Ice cream with strawberries

Ingredient

- 2 pints Strawberries

- ¼ cup Sugar

- ⅓cup Dry red wine

- 1 Whole cinnamon stick

- ⅛ teaspoon Pepper, freshly ground

- 1 pint Vanilla ice cream

- 4 Sprigs fresh mint for Garnish

a) If strawberries are small, cut in half; if large, cut in quarters.

b) Combine sugar, red wine and cinnamon stick in a large skillet; cook over medium high heat until sugar dissolves, about 3 minutes. Add strawberries and pepper; cook until berries soften slighty, 4 to 5 minutes.

c) Remove from heat, discrad cinnamon stick and divide berries and sauce among dishes; serve with vanilla ice cream and a sprig of mint, if desired.

32. Melon mousse in muskat wine

Ingredient

- 11 ounces Melon Flesh; Galia preferred

- $\frac{1}{2}$ cup Sweet Muskat wine

- $\frac{1}{2}$ cup Sugar

- 1 cup Heavy Cream

- $\frac{1}{2}$ cup Sugar

- $\frac{1}{2}$ cup Water

- Assorted fruits

- $1\frac{1}{2}$ tablespoon Gelatine

- 2 Egg whites

- 2 cups Sweet Muskat wine

- 1 Cinnamon stick

- 1 Vanilla pod

a) In a blender, process the melon flesh to a smooth puree.

b) Put the gelatine and $\frac{1}{2}$ cup Muskat wine in a small pan, and bring to a boil, mixing well to ensure that the gelatine is completely dissolved. Add the gelatine mixture to the pureed melon, and mix well. Put over a bowl full of ice cubes.

c) Meanwhile, whip the egg whites, adding the sugar gradually, until thick. Transfer the mousse to a bowl.

d) To make the sauce, put the sugar and water in a medium pan, bring to a boil and cook on low heat until it thickens and turns golden brown. Add 2 cups Muskat wine, cinnamon stick, vanilla pod, and a strip of orange peel. Boil.

33. Israeli wine and nut cake

Ingredient

- 8 Eggs

- 1½ cup   Granulated sugar

- ½ teaspoon   Salt

- ¼ cup   Orange juice

- 1 tablespoon   Orange rind

- ¼ cup   Red passover wine

- $1\frac{1}{4}$ cup   Matzoh cake meal

- 2 tablespoons   Potato starch

- $\frac{1}{2}$ teaspoon   Cinnamon

- ⅓cup   Almonds; very finely chopped

a) Gradually beat $1\frac{1}{4}$ cups sugar and salt into yolk mixture until very thick and light in color. Add orange juice, rind, and wine; beat at high speed until thick and light, about 3 minutes.

b) Sift together meal, potato starch, and cinnamon; gradually fold into orange mixture until smoothly blended. Beat egg whites at highest speed until whites stand in peaks but are not dry.

c) Fold meringue lightly into mixture. Fold nuts into batter gently.

d) Turn into ungreased 10 inch tube pan with bottom lined with waxed paper.

e) Bake at 325 degrees.

34. Wine biscuits

Yield: 12 Servings

Ingredient

- $1\frac{1}{4}$ cup   Flour

- 1 pinch   Salt

- 3 ounces Shortening; (Oleo)

- 2 ounces Sugar

- 1 Egg

- ¼ cup   Sherry; To 1/3 C,Or Any Wine

a) Prepare as you would for regular biscuits, that is: combine dry ingredients and cut in oleo. Combine egg and sherry and mix in to form a soft dough.

b) Pat out on a floured surface. Cut with biscuit cutter, place on baking sheets and sprinkle with a bit of sugar or flour. Bake 350, 8 to 10 minutes.

35. Gooseberry wine fondue

Ingredient

- 1½ pounds Gooseberries; topped and tailed

- 4 ounces Caster (granulated) sugar

- ⅔cup Dry white wine

- 2 teaspoons Cornflour (cornstarch)

- 2 tablespoons Single (light) cream

- Brandy snaps

a) Reserve a few gooseberries for decoration, then pass remainder through a sieve to make a puree.

b) In a fondue pot, blend corn flour smoothly with cream. Stir in gooseberry puree, then heat until smooth and thick, stirring frequently.

c) Decorate with reserved gooseberries and serve with brandy snaps.

36. Cake & wine pudding

Ingredient

- Macaroons

- 1 pint Wine

- 3 Egg yolk

- 3 Egg white

- Sponge cake

- Lady fingers

- 1 teaspoon Cornstarch

- 3 teaspoons Sugar

- ½ cup Nuts, chopped

a) Place pieces of sponge cake, lady fingers or similar cake into an earthenware dish (fill about ½ full). Add a few macaroons. Heat the wine. Mix the cornstarch and sugar together and slowly add the wine.

b) Beat the yolks of eggs and add to the wine mixture. Cook about 2 minutes. Pour over the cake and let cool. When cool, cover with the stiffly beaten egg whites and sprinkle with the chopped nutmeats.

c) Bake at 325-F for a few minutes to brown. Serve cold

37. Red wine and blueberry granita

Ingredient

- 4 cups Fresh blueberries

- 2 cups Sugar syrup

- 2 cups Burgandy or dry red wine

- $4\frac{1}{2}$ cup Sugar

- 4 cups Water

a) Strain Blueberries into large saucepan with sieve, discarding solids. Add syrup and wine, bring mixture to a boil, reduce heat, then let simmer, uncovered, 3-4 minutes. pour mixture into a 8 inch square dish, cover and freeze at least 8 hours or until firm.

b) Remove mixture from freezer, and scrape entire mixture with the tines of a fork until fluffy. Spoon into a container; cover and freeze for up to one month.

c) Basic Sugar Syrup: Combine in saucepan, stirring well. Bring to boil, cook until the sugar dissolves.

38. Melon and blueberry coupé

Ingredient

- 1½ cup Dry white wine

- ½ cup Sugar

- 1   Vanilla bean; split lengthwise

- 2⅓cup Cantaloupe cubes; (about 1/2 melon)

- 2⅓cup Honeydew cubes

- 2⅓cup   Watermelon cubes

- 3 cups Fresh blueberries

- $\frac{1}{2}$ cup Chopped fresh mint

a) Combine $\frac{1}{2}$ cup wine and sugar in small saucepan. Scrape in seeds from vanilla bean; add bean. Stir over low heat until sugar dissolves and syrup is hot, about 2 minutes. Remove from heat and let steep 30 minutes. Remove vanilla bean from syrup.

b) Combine all fruit in large bowl. Add mint and remaining 1 cup wine to sugar syrup. Pour over fruit. Cover and refrigerate at least 2 hours.

c) Spoon fruit and some syrup into large stemmed goblets.

39. Lime pie with wine cream

Ingredient

- 1¼ cup Chilled whipping cream

- 6 tablespoons Sugar

- 2 tablespoons Sweet dessert wine

- 1½ tablespoon Fresh lemon juice

- 1 tablespoon Finely chopped walnuts

- ¼ cup Sugar

- ½ teaspoon Salt

- ¾ cup chilled unsalted butter

- 2 large Egg yolks & 4 large Eggs

- ½ cup Fresh lime juice & 1 tablespoon Grated lime peel

a) Combine cream, sugar, wine and lemon juice in mixing bowl and beat until soft peaks form. Carefully fold in nuts.

b) Mix flour, sugar and salt in processor. Add butter; cut in using on/off turns until mixture resembles coarse meal. Whisk yolks and water in bowl. Add to processor; blend using on/off turns until moist clumps form. Bake 20 minutes.

c) Whisk eggs and sugar in bowl until light and creamy. Sift flour into egg mixture; whisk to combine. Add buttermilk. Melt butter with lime juice and Whisk into egg mixture. Pour filling into crust.

40. Matzoh-wine rolls

Ingredient

- 8 Squares matzoh

- 1 cup Sweet red wine

- 8 ounces Semi-sweet chocolate

- $\frac{1}{2}$ cup Milk

- 2 tablespoons Cocoa

- 1 cup Sugar

- 3 tablespoons Brandy

- 1 teaspoon Instant coffee powder

- 2 Sticks margarine

a) Crumble the matzoh and soak in the wine. Melt the chocolate with the milk, cocoa powder, sugar, brandy and coffee over very low heat.

b) Remove from heat and add the margarine. Stir until melted.

c) Add the matzoh to the chocolate mixture. Divide the mixture in two halves..Shape each half into a long roll and wrap tightly in aluminium foil. Refrigerate overnight, remove the aluminium foil and slice.

d) Place in paper four cups and serve.

41. Moustokouloura

Ingredient

- 3½ cup All-purpose flour plus extra for kneading

- 2 teaspoons Baking soda

- 1 tablespoon Freshly ground cinnamon

- 1 tablespoon Freshly ground cloves

- ¼ cup Mild olive oil

- 2 tablespoons Honey

- $\frac{1}{2}$ cup Greek wine must syrup

- $\frac{1}{2}$ Orange

- 1 cup Orange juice

a) Sift together the flour, baking soda, cinnamon, and cloves into a large bowl, making a well in the center.

b) In a smaller bowl, beat the olive oil with the honey, petimezi, grated orange zest, and $\frac{1}{2}$ the orange juice and pour into the well. Mix together to make a dough.

c) Turn onto a floured surface and knead for about 10 minutes until the dough is smooth but not stiff.

d) Break off pieces of dough, about 2 tablespoonfuls each, and roll into snakes about $\frac{1}{2}$-inch in diameter.

e) Bake in an oven preheated to 375 F for 10-15 minutes- until they are brown and crunchy, but not too hard.

42. Orange-wine wafers

Ingredient

- $2\frac{1}{2}$ tablespoon Orange zest

- 2 cups Pastry or all-purpose flour

- $\frac{1}{2}$ teaspoon Salt

- 1 teaspoon Baking powder

- 2 tablespoons (1/4 stick) butter or

- Margarine, softened

- $\frac{1}{2}$ cup White wine

a) Preheat the oven to 350~F.

b) To prepare the zest, lightly grate the outer peel of the oranges against the fine grate of a cheese grater.

c) In a large bowl combine the flour, orange zest, salt, and baking powder. Cut in the butter and slowly add the wine.

d) On a floured surface, fold the left third of the dough over the center third. Likewise, fold the right third over the center.

e) Roll the dough out somewhat thinner this time, about $\frac{1}{8}$ inch thick.

f) With a sharp knife, cut in to 2-inch squares.

g) Prick each cracker all the way through 2 or 3 times with the tines of a fork. Bake for 15 to 20 minutes, until lightly browned.

43. Orange almond cake

Ingredient

- ½ cup Unsalted butter - (1 stick); softened

- 1 cup Granulated sugar

- 2 Eggs

- 2 teaspoons Vanilla

- ½ teaspoon Almond extract

- ¼ cup Ground unblanched almonds

- 2 teaspoons Grated orange zest

- 1½ cup   All-purpose flour; plus

- 2 tablespoons   All-purpose flour

- 2 teaspoons Baking powder

- 1 teaspoon Salt

- 1 cup Sour cream

- 1 pint Raspberries or strawberries

- ½ cup Sparkling wine

a) Beat butter and sugar together until light and fluffy.

b) Add eggs, vanilla, almond extract, almonds and orange zest; beat on low until combined. Sift flour, baking powder and salt together; add alternately to butter mixture with sour cream.

c) Pour batter into pan; tap lightly to even it. Bake for about 20 minutes.

d) Let cool for 10 minutes; remove from cake pan or remove sides of springform. Sprinkle berries with sugar, then toss with enough sparkling wine to dampen them thoroughly.

e) Place cake on plate, surround with berries and juice.

44. Plum tart with creme fraiche

Ingredient

- 10 Inch sweet pastry shell; up to 11

- 550 grams Plums; washed

- 2 tablespoons Caster sugar

- 125 millilitres Port wine

- 1 Vanilla pod cut down the centre

- $\frac{1}{2}$ pint Cream

- 1 ounce Flour

- 2 ounces Sugar

- 2 Egg yolks

- 2 Leaf gelatine; soaked

a) Remove the stones from the plums and cut into four. Bake the sweet pastry case blind and cool.

b) Make the creme pat by mixing egg and sugar in a bowl over hot water. Add a tablespoon of cream and gradually add the flour. Add more cream and put in a clean pan and re-warm.

c) Place a good layer of creme pat on the base of the pastry case and smooth level with a palette knife or plastic scraper.

d) Arrange the plums on the pastry and bake in the oven for 30-40 minutes.

e) Simmer the sugar in the port wine and add the vanilla pod, reduce the liquid slightly. Add the leaf gelatine and cool slightly. Remove the tart and cool, pour over the port glaze and leave in the fridge to set. Slice and serve with creme fraiche.

45. Red Wine Brownies

INGREDIENTS

- ¾ cup (177 mL) red wine
- ½ cup (60 g) dried cranberries
- 1 ¼ (156 g) cups all-purpose flour
- ½ teaspoon sea salt
- ½ cup (115 g) salted butter, plus extra for greasing
- 6 oz (180 g) dark or semi-sweet chocolate
- 3 large eggs
- 1 ¼ cups (250 g) sugar
- ½ cup (41 g) unsweetened cocoa powder

- $\frac{1}{2}$ cup (63 g) chopped walnuts (optional)

Directions:

a) In a small bowl, mix the red wine and cranberries together and allow to sit for 30 minutes to an hour or until the cranberries look plump. You can gently heat the wine and cranberries on the stove or in the microwave to speed up the process.

b) Preheat oven to 350 degrees F. and grease and flour an 8 by 8 inch pan.

c) Mix flour and sea salt in a bowl and set aside.

d) In a bowl over boiling water, heat the butter and chocolate until just melted and mixed together.

e) Remove the bowl from heat and beat in the eggs one at a time. (If the bowl seems very hot, you may want to let it cool for about 5 minutes before adding the eggs).

46. Vanilla panna cotta

Ingredients

- Cream - 2 cups
- Sugar, plus 3 Tbsp - 1/4 cup
- Vanilla beans - both split in half, seeds scraped from one - 1
- Vanilla paste - 1/2 tsp
- Oil - 1 Tbsp
- Powdered gelatine mixed with 90ml cold water - 2 tsp
- Punnet strawberries - 125 g

- Red wine - 1/2 cup

Directions:

a) Gently heat the cream and 1/2 cup of sugar in a pot until all the sugar has dissolved. Remove from heat and stir in the vanilla extract and 1 vanilla bean along with the seeds scraped from it.

b) Sprinkle the gelatin over the cold water in a large bowl and gently combine.

c) Pour the warmed cream over the gelatin and combine thoroughly until the gelatin has dissolved. Strain the mix through a sieve.

d) Divide the mixture between the greased bowls and refrigerate until set. This will usually take up to 3 hours.

e) In a pot heat the red wine, 6 Tbsp of sugar and remaining vanilla bean until boiling.

f) Rinse, hull and slice the strawberries and add to the syrup,,then spoon over the released panna cotta.

47. Wine tart

Ingredient

- 140 grams Plain flour (5 oz)

- 1 teaspoon Baking powder

- 60 grams Unsalted butter (2 1/4 oz)

- 1 dash Salt

- 120 grams Caster sugar (4 oz)

- 1 teaspoon Ground cinnamon

- 10 grams Plain flour (1/4 oz)

- ½ teaspoon Sugar

- 3 tablespoons Milk

- 100 millilitres   Good dry white wine

- 15 grams Butter (approx. 1/2 oz)

a) Pastry: put the flour, baking powder and softened butter together in a large bowl. Add the salt and sugar. Add the milk.

b) Ease the pastry into the base of the tin.

c) Mix the sugar, cinnamon and flour together. Strew this mixture all over the bottom of the tart. Pour the wine over the sugar mixture and mix it with your fingertips.

d) Cook the tart in the bottom of the pre-heated oven for 15 ... 20 minutes.

e) Leave the tart to cool before taking it out of the tin.

48. Zabaglione

Ingredient

- 6 Egg yolks

- ½ cup   Sugar

- ⅓cup   Medium white wine

a) Beat egg yolks with electric mixer in top of
   double boiler until foamy. Beat in sugar
   gradually. Pour just enough hot water in bottom
   of double boiler so that top part does not
   touch water.

b) Cook egg yolks over medium heat; mix in wine slowly, beating on high speed until smooth, pale and thick enough to stand in soft mounds.

c) Serve immediately in shallow stemmed glasses.

49. Winter fruits in red wine

Ingredient

- 1 Lemon

- 500 millilitres Red wine

- 450 grams Caster sugar

- 1 Vanilla pod; halved

- 3 Bay leaves

- 1 Cinnamon stick

- 12 Black peppercorns

- 4 smalls Pears
- 12 No-soak prunes
- 12 No-soak apricots

a) Pare a strip of lemon zest and halve the lemon. Put the lemon zest, sugar, wine, vanilla pod, bay leaves and spices into a large non-reactive pan and boil, stirring.

b) Peel the pears and rub with the cut face of the lemon to stop discolouration. Bring the red wine syrup back to the boil, turn down to a gentle simmer and add the pears.

c) Add the prunes and apricots to the pears. Replace the lid and allow to cool completely before refrigerating overnight.

50. Lemon tea cake

Ingredient

- ½ cup Dry red wine

- 3 tablespoons Fresh lemon juice

- 1½ tablespoon Cornstarch

- 1 cup Fresh blueberries

- Pinch Ground cinnamon & nutmeg

- ½ cup Unsalted butter; room temperature

- 1 cup Sugar

- 3 large Eggs

- 2 tablespoons Grated lemon peel

- 2 tablespoon Fresh lemon juice

- 1 teaspoon Vanilla extract

- $1\frac{1}{2}$ cup Sifted cake flour

- $\frac{1}{2}$ teaspoon Baking powder & $\frac{1}{4}$ Baking soda

- $\frac{1}{4}$ teaspoon Salt

- $\frac{1}{2}$ cup Sour cream

a) Stir water, sugar, dry red wine, fresh lemon juice and cornstarch in medium saucepan.

b) Add blueberries. Boil until sauce thickens enough to coat back of spoon, stirring constantly, about 5 minutes.

c) Beat butter and sugar in large bowl until fluffy. Beat in eggs, 1 at a time. Beat in grated lemon peel, lemon juice and vanilla extract. Sift cake flour, baking powder, baking soda and salt into medium bowl.

d) Pour batter into prepared baking pan. Bake and then cool cake on rack 10 minutes.

INFUSED MAIN DISHES

51. Wine & Saffron Infused Mussels

INGREDIENTS

- 2 onions, peeled and halved
- 2 red chillies, stem removed
- 2 tbs olive oil
- 1/2 tsp saffron threads, soaked in 2 tablespoons hot water
- 300ml dry white wine
- 500ml fish stock
- 2 tbs tomato paste

- Sea salt flakes and freshly ground black pepper
- 1kg fresh mussels, beards removed and cleaned
- Several thyme sprigs

Directions:

a) Add the onions and chillies to processor.

b) Place the pan over a medium low heat, add the onions and chillies and cook stirring for 5 minutes until the onions glisten and soften

c) Add the saffron thread mixture and cook 30 seconds. Add the wine, fish stock, tomato paste and season well with the salt and pepper. Bring to the boil, reduce the heat to low and simmer 5 minutes

d) Increase the heat to high, when the sauce is boiling add the mussels and thyme sprigs. Cover with the lid and cook 3-5 minutes, shaking the pan occasionally, until the mussels steam open

e) Serve immediately with crusty bread

52. Scallops in wine sauce

Ingredient

- 2 pounds Sea scallops

- 2 tablespoons   Olive oil

- ¼ tablespoon   Hot pepper flakes

- 2   Cloves garlic; finely chopped

- 1 tablespoon   White wine

- 1 tablespoon   Curry powder

- 1 small   Tomato; peeled, seeded and chopped

- $\frac{1}{4}$ cup   Heavy cream

- 2 tablespoons Tabasco sauce

- Salt and pepper to taste

- 1 tablespoon Parsley; finely chopped

a) Pour some olive oil into one of the skillets on the range top. Then, add the red pepper flakes, garlic and white wine. Add all of the sea scallops to the skillet. Cover the pan and let the scallops cook over med/high heat until the scallops become firm and opaque.

b) Remove the pan from the heat and transfer the scallops to a large serving bowl. Add 1 tbsp. oil and the curry powder to a small saucepan and cook for 1-2 minutes.

c) Add the reserved scallop liquid to the saucepan of oil and curry by straining $\frac{3}{4}$ cup of it through cheesecloth or a coffee filter. To the same saucepan, add the tomato pieces, cream, Tabasco, salt, pepper and parsley, and heat for 2 to 3 minutes.

.

53. Halibut steaks with wine sauce

Ingredient

- 3 tablespoons Shallots; chopped

- $1\frac{1}{2}$ pounds Halibut steaks; 1 inch thick, cut into 4 in. piece

- 1 cup Dry white wine

- 2 mediums Plum tomatoes; chopped

- $\frac{1}{2}$ teaspoon Dried tarragon

- $\frac{1}{4}$ teaspoon Salt

- $\frac{1}{8}$ teaspoon Pepper

- 2 tablespoons Olive oil

a) Preheat oven to 450 degrees. Sprinkle shallots over bottom of a 1-$\frac{1}{2}$ to 2-quart baking dish. Place fish in shallow baking pan and pour in wine.

b) Sprinkle chopped tomato, tarragon, salt, and pepper over fish. Drizzle with oil.

c) Bake 10 to 12 minutes, until fish is opaque throughout. Remove fish with a slotted spatula to a serving dish and peel off skin.

d) Set baking pan (if metal) over a stove burner or pour liquid and vegetables into a small saucepan. Boil over high heat until sauce reduces slightly, 1 to 2 minutes. Spoon sauce over fish and serve.

54. Greek meat rolls in wine sauce

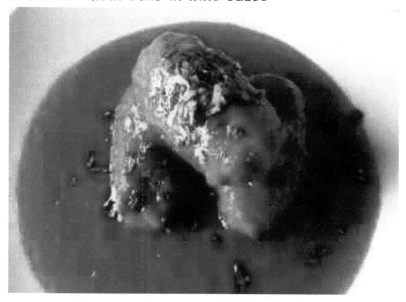

Ingredient

- 2 pounds Lean ground beef or turkey

- 4 slices Dry white toast, crumbled

- Onion & Garlic

- 1 Egg, slightly beaten

- 1 tablespoon Sugar

- Pinch Salt, Cumin, Black Pepper

- Flour (about 1/2 C.)

- 1 can (12-oz) tomato paste

- 1½ cup Dry red wine

- 2 teaspoons Salt

- Steamed rice

- Chopped parsley

a) Mix dry ingredients until well-blended and firm.

b) Moisten hands in cold water and shaped tablespoonfuls of the meat mixture into rolls (logs) about 2-½" to 3" long. Coat each roll lightly with flour.

c) In a deep skillet, heat about ½" oil and brown rolls a few at a time, taking care not to crowd them. Remove browned rolls to paper towels to drain.

d) In a Dutch oven, whisk together tomato paste, water, wine, salt, and cumin. Add meat rolls to sauce. Cover and simmer for 45 minutes to one hour, until meat rolls are done through. Taste sauce and add salt if necess ary.

55. Lentils with glazed vegetables

Ingredient

- 1½ cup French green lentils; sorted & rinsed

- 1½ teaspoon Salt; divided

- 1   Bay leaf

- 2 teaspoons Olive oil

- Onion, celery, garlic

- 1 tablespoon Tomato paste

- ⅔cup Dry red wine

- 2 teaspoons Dijon mustard

- 2 tablespoons Butter or extra-virgin olive oil

- Freshly ground pepper to taste

- 2 teaspoons Fresh parsley

a) Put lentils in a saucepan with 3 cups water, 1 tsp. salt, and the bay leaf. Bring to a boil.

b) Meanwhile, heat the oil in a medium skillet. Add the onion, carrot, and celery, season with $\frac{1}{2}$ tsp. salt, and cook over medium-high heat, stirring frequently, until the vegetables are browned, about 10 minutes. Add the garlic and tomato paste, cook for 1 minute more, and then add the wine.

c) Bring to a boil, and then lower the heat and simmer, covered, until the liquid is syrupy.

d) Stir in the mustard and add the cooked lentils along with their broth.

e) Simmer until the sauce is mostly reduced, then stir in the butter and season with pepper.

56. Halibut in vegetable sauce

Ingredient

- 2 pounds Halibut

- $\frac{1}{4}$ cup Flour

- $\frac{1}{2}$ teaspoon Salt

- White pepper

- 1 tablespoon Chopped parsley

- $\frac{1}{4}$ cup Olive oil

- 1 Crushed garlic clove

- 1 Chopped large onion

- 1 Grated carrot

- 2 Stalks chopped celery

- 1 large Chopped tomato

- $\frac{1}{4}$ cup Water

- $\frac{3}{4}$ cup Dry white wine

a) Combine flour, salt, pepper & parsley: dredge fish with flour mixture. Heat olive oil in skillet; add halibut & fry until golden brown on both sides.

b) Remove from skillet & set aside. Add garlic, onion, carrot & celery to skillet: sauté' 10-15 minutes, until tender. Add tomato & water, simmer 10 minutes.

c) Remove sauce from heat & pour into blender; puree. Stir in wine. Return to skillet: place fish in sauce. Cover & simmer 5 minutes.

57. Herbed sausages in wine

Ingredient

- $\frac{1}{2}$ pounds Italian Sweet Sausage

- $\frac{1}{2}$ pounds Italian Hot Sausage

- $\frac{1}{2}$ pounds Lielbasa

- $\frac{1}{2}$ pounds Bockwurst (Veal Sausage)

- 5 Green Onions, Minced

- 2 cups Dry White Wine

- 1 tablespoon Chopped Fresh Thyme Leaves

- 1 tablespoon Finely Chopped Fresh Parsley

- $\frac{1}{2}$ teaspoon Tabasco Pepper Sauce

a) Cut the sausages into $\frac{1}{2}$-inch pieces. In a deep skillet over medium heat, cook the Italian sausage for 3 to 5 minutes, or until lightly browned. Drain off the fat. Add the remaining sausage and the green onions, and cook for 5 minutes more.

b) Reduce the heat to low, add the remaining ingredients, and simmer for 20 minutes, stirring occasionally. Serve immediately, or keep warm in a chafing dish. Serve with toothpicks.

58. Fish rolls in white wine

Ingredient

- ⅔cup Seedless green grapes, Halved

- ¾ cup Dry white wine

- Four; (6 to 8-ounce)

- skinless flounder

- ⅓cup Minced fresh parsley leaves

- 1 tablespoon Minced fresh thyme

- ¼ cup Minced onion

- 2 tablespoons Unsalted butter

- 1 tablespoon All-purpose flour

- $\frac{1}{4}$ cup Heavy cream

- 1 teaspoon Fresh lemon juice

a) In a small saucepan let the grape halves macerate in the wine for 1 hour.

b) Halve the fillets lengthwise, season them with salt and pepper, and sprinkle the skinned sides with the parsley and the thyme. Roll up each fillet half with 1 of the reserved grapes in the middle and secure it with a wooden pick.

c) In a small saucepan cook the onion in the butter, stir in the flour, and cook the roux.

d) Add the cream, the macerated grapes, the lemon juice, and salt and pepper to taste and boil the sauce, stirring for 3 minutes.

e) Pour off any liquid that has accumulated on the plate, divide the fish rolls among 4 heated plates, and spoon the sauce over them.

59. Herbed tofu in white wine sauce

Ingredient

- 2 tablespoons (soy) margarine

- 1½ tablespoon Flour

- ½ cup   (soy) milk

- ½ cup   White wine

- 1 Wedge of onion left in one

- Piece (I can't tolerate much

- Onion, so I

- Used about a 4cm x 2cm

- Wedge)

- 1 dash   Ground cloves

- 1 dash   Salt

- x Some water

- ½ pounds Or so herbed tofu, cubed

- (about 1.5 cm cubes)

- x Your favorite pasta, enough

a) Melt margarine in pan and wisk in flour. Cool a bit and then wisk in wine and (soy)milk.

b) Add onion, cloves, and salt to sauce and stir over low heat until sauce is slightly thickened. If it gets too thick, add some water. Add tofu and simmer while you cook the pasta.

c) Serve tofu and sauce over pasta, giving the onion to the person who likes them more.

60. Grilled octopus in red wine marinade

Ingredient

- 2 Cleaned 1 1/2 pound octopus

- Carrots, Celery & Onion

- 2 Bay leaves

- 2 teaspoons Salt

- Whole black peppercorns & Dried thyme

- 2 cups Red wine

- 3 tablespoons Extra-virgin olive oil

- 3 tablespoons Red wine vinegar

- 3 tablespoons Dry red wine

- Salt, Fresh ground black pepper

- 1⅓cup Strained octopus cooking broth

- ¼ cup Extra-virgin olive oil

- 1 tablespoon Lemon juice

- 2 tablespoons Butter

a) In a large casserole combine octopus, carrots, celery, onion, bay leaves, salt, pepper, thyme, red wine and water. Bring to a slow boil.

b) Make marinade: in a small bowl combine marinade ingredients. Pour over octopus and toss to coat.

c) Make sauce: in a small saucepan combine strained reserved broth, olive oil, lemon juice and vinegar. Stir in parsley.

d) Grill 4 minutes, turning frequently, until lightly charred and heated through. Seve.

61. Baked sweet plantains in wine

Ingredient

- 4 eaches Very ripe plantains

- 1 cup   Olive oil

- ½ cup   Brown sugar

- ½ teaspoon   Ground cinnamon

- 1 cup   Sherry wine

a) Preheat oven to 350F. Remove peel from
   plantains and slice them lengthwise in half. In a

large sauté pan, heat oil to medium hot and add plantains.

b) Cook them until lightly browned on each side. Place them in a large baking dish and sprinkle sugar over all. Add cinnamon and cover with wine. Bake for 30 minutes, or until they take on a reddish hue.

62. Pasta in lemon and white wine sauce

Ingredient

- 1½ pounds Pasta; your choice

- 1 Full chicken breast; cooked, julienne

- 10 ounces Asparagus; blanched

- ¼ cup Butter

- ½ small Onion

- 4 tablespoons All-purpose flour

- 2 cups Dry white wine

- 2 cups Chicken broth

- 12 teaspoons Lemon zest

- 1 tablespoon Fresh thyme; chopped

- 1 tablespoon Fresh dill; chopped

- 3 tablespoons Dijon mustard

- Salt and pepper; to taste

- Parmesan cheese; grated

a) Cook pasta and hold Cook chicken breast and blanch asparagus; hold. Warm the butter in a large saucepan over medium-low heat. Add the onion and sauté ,until lightly brown and very soft.

b) Add the flour and reduce the heat to low. Stir until completely blended. Very gradually whisk in the white wine and broth.

c) Bring the sauce to a boil and then let simmer for 10 minutes. Stir in the lemon zest, thyme, dill, mustard and season to taste with salt and white pepper. Add the cooked and julienne chicken and asparagus.

63. Pasta with mussels in wine

Ingredient

- 1 pounds Mussels (in their shells)

- White wine (enough to fill a large shallow saucepan about 1/2 an inch)

- 2 larges Cloves garlic, finely chopped

- 2 tablespoons Olive oil

- 1 teaspoon Freshly ground pepper

- 3 tablespoons Chopped fresh basil

- 1 large   Tomato, coarsely chopped

- 2 pounds Pasta

a) Thoroughly wash the mussels, pulling off all beards, and scraping shells as necessary. Place in saucepan with wine.

b) Cover tightly and steam until the shells open While the mussels cool a bit, put wine broth over medium heat and add garlic, olive oil, pepper, tomato, and basil.

c) Pour sauce over hot linguini or fettucini and serve!

64. Red wine fettucine and olives

Ingredient

- 2½ cup   Flour

- 1 cup   Semolina flour

- 2 Eggs

- cup   Dry red wine

- 1 Recipe lumache alla marchigiana

a) To Prepare Pasta: Make a well of the flour and putting the eggs and wine in the center.

b) Using a fork, beat together the eggs and wine and begin to incorporate the flour starting with the inner rim of the well.

c) Start kneading the dough with both hands, using the palms of your hands.

d) Roll out pasta to thinnest setting on pasta machine. Cut pasta into $\frac{1}{4}$ inch thick noodles by hand or with machine and set aside under a moist towel.

e) Bring 6 quarts water to boil and add 2 tablespoons salt. Heat snail to boil and set aside.

f) Drop pasta into water and cook until just tender. Drain pasta and put into pan with snails, tossing well to coat. Serve immediately in a warm serving dish.

65. Orecchiette pasta & chicken

Ingredient

- 6 larges Chicken Thighs, boned & skinned

- Salt And Freshly Ground Black Pepper, to taste

- 2 tablespoons Olive Or Canola Oil

- ½ pounds Fresh Shiitake Mushrooms

- Onion, Garlic, Carrots & Celery

- 2 cups Hearty Red Wine

- 2 cups Ripe Tomatoes, diced, seeded

- 1 teaspoon Fresh Thyme/Fresh Sage

- 4 cups Chicken Stock

- ⅓ cup Finely Chopped Parsley

- ½ pounds Orecchiette Pasta, uncooked

- ¼ cup Chopped Fresh Basil

- ¼ cup Drained Sundried Tomatoes

- Fresh Basil Sprigs

- Freshly Shaved Asiago Or Parmesan Cheese

a) Season chicken & quickly brown chicken over high heat.

b) Add mushrooms, onion, garlic, carrots, and celery and sauté until very lightly browned. Return chicken to pan and add wine, tomatoes, thyme, sage, and the stock and bring to a simmer. Stir in parsley and keep warm.

c) Prepare pasta & Serve. Garnish with basil springs and shaved cheese.

66. Beef with portobello sauce

Ingredient

- 500 grams Lean ground beef

- $\frac{1}{2}$ Dry red wine

- $\frac{1}{2}$ teaspoon Pepper; coarse ground

- 4 tablespoons Roquefort or stilton cheese

- $\frac{3}{4}$ pounds Portobellos; (375g or 4 med)

a) Brown meat from 2-4 minutes per side

b) Pour in ½ cup of the wine and generously grind pepper over patties.

c) Reduce heat to medium and simmer, uncovered, for 3 minutes. Turn patties, crumble cheese over top and continue simmering uncovered until cheese begins to melt, about 3 minutes.

d) Meanwhile, separate stems from mushroom caps. Thickly slice stems and caps.

e) Add mushrooms to wine in pan and Stir constantly until they are hot.

f) Spoon mushrooms around patties, then pour sauce over top.

67. Italian cheese and red wine sausage

Ingredient

- 4 pounds Pork, boneless, shoulder or butt

- 1 tablespoon   Fennel seed, ground in mortar

- 2 Bay leaves, crushed

- $\frac{1}{4}$ cup   Parsley, chopped

- 5 Garlic, pressed

- $\frac{1}{2}$ teaspoon   Pepper, red, flakes

- 3 teaspoons   Salt, kosher

- 1 teaspoon Pepper, black, freshly ground

- 1 cup Cheese, parmesan or romano, grated

- ¾ cup Wine, red

- 4 Sausage casings (about

a) Grind the meat in food processor or Kitchen Aid meat grinder attachment for mixer. Mix all ingredients and allow to stand for 1 hour so flavours can meld.

b) Stuff sausage into casings with Kitchen Aid sausage stuffing attachment or buy hand with sausage funnel.

68. Mushrooms & tofu in wine

Ingredient

- 1 tablespoon Safflower oil

- 2 eaches Garlic cloves, minced

- 1 large Onion, chopped

- 1½ pounds Mushrooms, sliced

- ½ medium Green bell pepper, diced

- ½ cup Dry white wine

- ¼ cup Tamari

- ½ teaspoon Grated ginger

- 2 teaspoons   Sesame oil

- 1½ tablespoon   Cornstarch

- 2 eaches Cakes tofu, grated

- Crushed almonds

a) Heat safflower in a wok. When hot add garlic & onion & saute over moderately low heat till the onion is translucent. Add mushrooms, bell pepper, wine, tamari, ginger & sesame oil. Mix.

b) Dissolve cornstarch in a small amount of water & stir into skillet.

c) Stir in tofu, cover & simmer for another 2 minutes.

69. Apricot-wine soup

Ingredient

- 32 ounces Canned apricots; undrained

- 8 ounces Sour cream

- 1 cup Chablis or dry white wine

- $\frac{1}{4}$ cup Apricot liqueur

- 2 tablespoons Lemon juice

- 2 teaspoons Vanilla extract

- $\frac{1}{4}$ teaspoon Ground cinnamon

a) Combine all ingredients in container of electric blender or food processor, process until smooth.

b) Cover and chill thoroughly. Ladle soup into individual soup bowls. Garnish with additional sour cream and ground cinnamon.

70. Mushroom soup with red wine

Ingredient

- 50G; (2-3oz) butter, (50 to 75)

- 1 large   Onion; chopped

- 500 grams   Button mushrooms; sliced (1lb)

- 300 millilitres Dry red wine; (1/2 pint)

- 900 millilitres Vegetable stock; (1 1/2 pints)

- 450 millilitres Double cream; (3/4 pint)

- A small bunch of fresh parsley; chopped finely, to garnish

a) Melt 25g (1oz) butter in a small frying-pan over a medium-low heat and fry the onion for 2-3 minutes, until just soft, stirring frequently.

b) Heat another 25g (1oz) butter in a large saucepan over a medium-low heat.

c) Add the mushrooms and fry them for 8-10 minutes, until soft.

d) Add the wine and cook for a further 5 minutes. Add the stock and onion, and simmer gently, without boiling, over a low heat, for 15 minutes.

e) When ready to serve, reheat the soup gently over a low heat and stir in the cream.

71. Borleves (wine soup)

Ingredient

- 4 cups   Red or white wine

- 2 cups   Water

- 1 teaspoon   Grated lemon rind

- 8 eaches Cloves

- 1 each   Stick of cinnamon

- 3 eaches Egg yolks

- $\frac{3}{4}$ cup   Sugar

a) Pour the wine and water into the saucepan. Add the grated lemon rind, the cloves and the cinnamon. Simmer over low heat for 30 minutes.

b) Remove from the heat and discard the cloves and cinnamon stick. In the small mixing bowl, beat the egg yolks with a wire whisk. Add the sugar a little at a time and continue beating until thick. Stir the egg yolk mixture into the hot soup.

c) Return the saucepan to the heat and bring to the simmering point. Do not allow the soup to boil or the egg yolks will scramble. Serve in hot mugs.

72. Cherry-wine soup

Ingredient

- 1 ounce   Can pitted tart red cherries

- 1½ cup   Water

- ½ cup   Sugar

- 1 tablespoon   Quick-cooking tapioca

- $\frac{1}{8}$ teaspoon   Ground cloves

- $\frac{1}{2}$ cup   Dry red wine

a) In $1\frac{1}{2}$-quart saucepan stir together undrained cherries, water, sugar, tapioca, and cloves. Let stand 5 minutes. Bring to boiling.

b) Reduce heat; cover and simmer for 15 minutes, stirring occasionally.

c) Remove from heat; stir in wine. Cover and chill, stirring occasionally. Makes 6 to 8 servings.

73. Danish apple soup

Ingredient

- 2 larges Apples, cored, pared

- 2 cups Water

- 1   Cinnamon (2") stick

- 3 Whole cloves

- $\frac{1}{8}$ teaspoon Salt

- $\frac{1}{2}$ cup Sugar

- 1 tablespoon Cornstarch

- 1 cup Fresh prune plums, unpeeled & sliced

- 1 cup Fresh peaches, peeled and cut

- $\frac{1}{4}$ cup Port wine

a) Combine apples, water, cinnamon stick, cloves, and salt in a medium-large saucepan.

b) Blend together the sugar and cornstarch and add to pureed apple mixture.

c) Add the plums and peaches and simmer just until these fruits are tender and the mixture has thickened slightly.

d) Add the port wine.

e) Top individual servings with a dollop of light sour cream or non-fat vanilla yogurt.

74. Cranberry wine jello salad

Ingredient

- 1 large Pkg. rasberry jello

- 1¼ cup Boiling water

- 1 large Can whole cranberry sauce

- 1 large Can undrained crushed

- Pineapple

- 1 cup Chopped nuts

- ¾ cup   Port wine

- 8 ounces Cream cheese

- 1 cup   Sour cream

- Dissolve jello in boiling water. Stir cranberry sauce in thoroughly.

a) Add pineapple, nuts and wine. Pour into a 9x 13 inch glass dish and chill for 24 hrs.

b) When ready to serve, stir cream cheese until soft, add sour cream and beat well. spread on top of Jello.

75. Dijon mustard with herbs and wine

Ingredient

- 1 cup Dijon mustard

- $\frac{1}{2}$ teaspoon Basil

- $\frac{1}{2}$ teaspoon Tarragon

- $\frac{1}{4}$ cup Red wine

a) Mix all ingredients.

b) Refrigerate overnight to blend flavours before using. Store in refrigerator.

76. Wine Infused Bucatini

Ingredients

- 2 tablespoons olive oil, divided
- 4 spicy Italian Style Pork Sausages
- 1 large shallot, sliced
- 4 cloves garlic, minced
- 1 tablespoon smoked paprika
- 1 pinch cayenne pepper
- 1 pinch crushed red pepper flakes
- Salt, to taste
- 2 cups dry white wine,
- 1 (14.5 ounce) can Roasted Diced Tomatoes

- 1 pound bucatini
- 1 tablespoon unsalted butter
- 1/ 2 cup freshly grated Parmesan cheese
- 1/ 2 cup chopped fresh parsley

Directions:

a) In a large pot or dutch oven, heat 1 tablespoon of olive oil over medium heat. Add sausage and cook until browned, about 8 minutes.

b) Add garlic and cook one minute more. When garlic is fragrant and golden brown add the smoked paprika, cayenne pepper and red pepper flakes. Season with salt and pepper.

c) Deglaze the pan with the wine, scraping any brown bits from the bottom of the pan.

d) Add the Fire Roasted Diced Tomatoes and water and bring to a simmer. Add the bucatini and cook.

e) When the pasta is cooked, stir in the reserved sausage, butter, Parmesan cheese and chopped parsley.

f) Season to taste with salt and pepper and enjoy!

77. Asparagus in wine

Ingredient

- 2 pounds Asparagus

- Boiling water

- ¼ cup Butter

- ¼ cup White wine

- ½ teaspoon Salt

- ¼ teaspoon Pepper

a) Wash asparagus and snap off ends. Lay spears in shallow pan and cover with salted boling water to cover. Bring to a boil and simmer for 8 minutes.

b) Drain and turn into buttered ramekins. Melt butter and stir in wine. Pour over asparagus. Sprinkle with salt and pepper and cheese. Bake at 425' for 15 minutes.

78. Mustard, wine marinated game chops

Ingredient

- 4 Caribou or Deer chops

- $\frac{1}{4}$ teaspoon Pepper

- 1 teaspoon Salt

- 3 tablespoons Stone ground mustard

- 1 cup red wine

a) Rub chops with mustard. Sprinkle with salt and pepper. Cover with wine and marinate overnight in refrigerator.

b) Broil or charcoal grill to medium rare basting with the marinade.

79. Chicken wings with wine dressing

Ingredient

- 8 Chicken wings

- ¼ cup Cornstarch

- 2 teaspoons Salt

- 1 cup Olive oil

- 1 cup Tarragon wine vinegar

- ¾ cup Dry white wine

- ½ teaspoon Dry mustard

- Dried basil, Tarragon, Oregano & white pepper

- Oil for frying

- Salt, pepper

- 1 small Tomato

- $\frac{1}{2}$ medium Green bell pepper

- $\frac{1}{2}$ small   Onion thinly sliced in rings

a) Dredge chicken in cornstarch mixed with 2 teaspoons salt and white pepper.

b) Heat oil to depth of $\frac{1}{2}$ inch in heavy skillet and fry chicken until golden brown and tender, about 7 minutes on each side.

c) To make dressing, combine oil, vinegar, wine, garlic, mustard, sugar, basil, oregano and tarragon. Season to taste with salt and pepper.

d) Combine tomato slices, green pepper and onion slices with dressing and mix well.

80. Oeufs en meurette

Ingredient

- Shallots; 6 peeled

- 2½ cup Beaujolais wine; plus

- 1 tablespoon Beaujolais wine

- 2.00 White mushrooms; quartered

- 3.00 slice Bacon; 2 coarsely chopped

- 4.00 slice French bread

- 3.00 tablespoon Butter; softened

- 2.00 Garlic cloves; 1 whole, smashed,
- Plus 1 finely minced
- 1.00 Bay leaf
- $\frac{1}{2}$ cup Chicken stock
- $1\frac{1}{4}$ tablespoon Flour
- 1.00 tablespoonRed wine vinegar
- 4.00 large Eggs
- 1.00 tablespoonParsley

a) Roast shallots until well-browned, basting them with $\frac{1}{2}$ cup of the wine. Add mushrooms to pan; place under hot broiler for 5 minutes, add coarsely-chopped bacon and broil.

b) Prepare croutes: Rub bread slices with smashed garlic clove and place on baking sheet. Broil.

c) Poach eggs 2 minutes until just set.

d) Pour sauce over eggs, sprinkle with parsley and serve immediately.

81. Red wine and mushroom risotto

Ingredient

- 1 ounce Porcini mushrooms; dried

- 2 cups Boiling water

- 1½ pounds Mushrooms; cremini or white

- 6 tablespoons Unsalted butter

- 5½ cup Chicken broth

- 6 ounces Pancetta; 1/4 inch thick

- 1 cup Onion; chopped fine

- Fresh rosemary & sage

- 3 cups Arborio rice

- 2 cups Dry red wine

- 3 tablespoons Fresh parsley; chopped fine

- 1 cup Parmesan cheese; freshly

a) In a small bowl, soak porcini in boiling water 30 minutes.

b) Cook pancetta over moderate heat. Add reserved finely chopped cremini or white mushrooms, remaining tablespoons butter, onion, rosemary, sage, and salt and pepper to taste while stirring until onion is softened. Stir in rice and cook.

c) Add 1 cup simmering broth and cook, stirring constantly, until absorbed.

82. Red wine gazpacho

Ingredient

- 2 slices White bread

- 1 cup   Cold water; more if needed

- 1 pounds Very ripe large tomatoes

- 1 Red pepper

- 1 mediumCucumber

- 1 Clove garlic

- $\frac{1}{4}$ cup   Olive oil

- $\frac{1}{2}$ cup   Red wine

- 3 tablespoons   Red wine vinegar; more if needed

- Salt and pepper

- 1 Pinches sugar

- Ice cubes; (for serving)

a) Put the bread in a small bowl, pour over the water and let soak. Core the tomatoes, cut them crosswise and scoop out the seeds. Cut the flesh in large chunks.

b) Puree the vegetables in the food processor in two batches, adding the olive oil and soaked bread to the last batch. Stir in the wine, vinegar, salt, pepper and sugar.

c) Spoon into bowls, add an ice cube and top with a knotted strip of cucumber peel.

83. Rice & vegetables in wine

Ingredient

- 2 tablespoons Oil

- 1 each   Onion, chopped

- 1 mediumZucchini, chopped

- 1 mediumCarrot, chopped

- 1 each   Stalk celery, chopped

- 1 cup   Long grain rice

- 1¼ cup   Vegetable stock

- 1 cup   White wine

a) Heat the oil in saucepan and saute the onion. Add the rest of the veggies and stir them over a medium heat, until lightly browned.

b) Add the rice, veg stock and white wine, cover and cook 15-20 minutes until all the liquid has been absorbed.

84. Baby salmon stuffed with caviar

Ingredient

- ½ cup Oil, olive

- 1 pounds Bones, salmon

- 1 pounds Butter

- 2 cups   Mirepoix

- 4 Bay leaves

- Oregano, Thyme, Peppercorns, white

- 4 tablespoons Puree, shallot

- $\frac{1}{4}$ cup Cognac

- 2 cups Wine, red

- 1 cup Stock, fish

a) In a saute pan, heat the olive oil.

b) Add the salmon bones to the pan and saute for about 1 minute.

c) Add butter (about 2 tablespoons), 1 cup mirepoix, 2 bay leaves, $\frac{1}{4}$ teaspoon of thyme, $\frac{1}{4}$ teaspoon of peppercorns, and 2 tablespoons of the shallot puree. Add cognac and flame.

d) Deglaze with 1 cup of red wine and cook over high heat for 5 to 10 minutes.

e) Melt butter. Add 2 tablespoons shallot puree, 1 cup mirepoix, 2 bay leaves, $\frac{1}{4}$ teaspoon peppercorns, $\frac{1}{4}$ teaspoon oregano, $\frac{1}{4}$ teaspoon thyme, and 3 cups of red wine.

f) Deglaze Strain and reserve.

85. Garlic-wine rice pilaf

Ingredient

- 1 Rind Of 1 Lemon

- 8 Cloves Garlic, Peeled

- $\frac{1}{2}$ cup Parsley

- 6 tablespoons   Unsalted Butter

- 1 cup Regular Rice (Not Instant)

- $1\frac{1}{4}$ cup Chicken Stock

- $\frac{3}{4}$ cup Dry Vermouth

- 1 Salt & Pepper To Taste

a) Chop together the lemon rind, garlic and parsley.

b) Heat the butter in heavy 2-qt pot. Cook the garlic mixture very gently for 10 minutes. Stir in the rice.

c) Stir over medium heat for 2 minutes. Combine the stock and wine in a saucepan. Stir into rice; add salt and freshly ground pepper.

d) Drape a towel over the pot and cover the towel until it is time to serve.

e) Serve hot or at room temperature.

86. Basque lamb's liver with red wine sauce

Ingredient

- 1 cup Dry red wine

- 1 tablespoon Red wine vinegar

- 2 teaspoons Minced fresh garlic

- 1   Bay leaf

- $\frac{1}{4}$ teaspoon Salt

- 1 pounds Lamb's liver

- 3 tablespoons Spanish olive oil

- 3 slices Bacon, chopped

- 3 tablespoons Finely chopped Italian

- Parsley

a) Combine wine, vinegar, garlic, bay, and salt in glass baking dish. Add liver and coat well with marinade.

b) Add bacon and cook until browned and crisp. Drain on paper towels.

c) Remove liver from marinade and pat dry. Brown liver in pan drippings for 2 minutes on each side. Remove to heated platter.

d) Pour marinade into hot skillet and boil, uncovered, until reduced by half. Scatter bacon pieces over liver, pour marinade on top and sprinkle with parsley.

87. Beef braised in barolo wine

Ingredient

- 2 Garlic clove, chopped

- 3½ pounds Beef, bottom round or chuck

- Salt, Pepper

- 2 Bay leaves, fresh or dried

- Thyme, dried, pinch

- 5 cups Wine, Barolo

- 3 tablespoons Butter

- 2 tablespoons Olive oil

- 1 Onion, medium, finely chopped

- 1 Carrot, finely chopped

- 1 Celery stalk, finely chopped

- $\frac{1}{2}$ pounds Mushrooms, white

a) Rub garlic into meat. Season with salt and pepper. Place meat in a large bowl. Add bay leaves, thyme and enough wine to cover meat.

b) Melt 2 tablespoons butter with oil in a large heavy casserole. When butter foams, add meat. Brown meat on all sides over medium heat.

c) Remove meat from casserole. Add onion, carrot and celery to casserole. Sauté until lightly browned. Return meat to casserole. Pour reserved marinade through a strainer over meat.

d) Melt 1 tablespoon butter in a medium skillet. Sauté mushrooms over high heat until golden. Add mushrooms to meat and cook 5 minutes longer.

88. Braised scrod in white wine

Ingredient

- $\frac{3}{4}$ cup olive oil; plus

- 2.00 tablespoon olive oil

- $1\frac{1}{2}$ pounds scrod fillets; cut 2x 2 pieces

- $\frac{1}{4}$ cup flour for dredging; seasoned with

- 1.00 teaspoon bayou blast

- 1.00 teaspoon chopped garlic

- $\frac{1}{2}$ cup pear or cherry tomatoes

- $\frac{1}{4}$ cup Kalamata olives; sliced

- 2.00 cup loosely packed oregano leaves

- $\frac{1}{4}$ cup dry white wine

- 1.00 teaspoon chopped lemon zest

a) Dredge fish pieces in the seasoned flour, shaking off the excess.

b) Carefully place all the fish pieces in the hot oil, and cook for 2 minutes.

c) In a large sauté pan heat the remaining 2 tablespoons olive oil over medium heat. Add chopped garlic and cook for 30 seconds. Place the fish in the pan with tomatoes, Kalamata olives, fresh oregano, white wine, lemon zest, water, and salt and pepper.

d) Cover and cook for 5 minutes over medium heat. Serve the sauce ladled over the fish.

89. Calamari in umido

Ingredient

- 16 smalls Calamari, fresh
- $\frac{1}{4}$ cup Olive oil, extra virgin
- 1 tablespoon Onion; chopped
- $\frac{1}{2}$ tablespoon Garlic; chopped
- $\frac{1}{4}$ teaspoon Red pepper; crushed
- $\frac{1}{3}$ cup Chardonnay
- $\frac{1}{4}$ cup Fish stock

- 3 eaches Parsley sprigs, Italian; chopped

- Salt, Pepper

a) Clean and peel the squid if this has not already been done by the fish market. Heat the olive oil in a skillet over medium heat.

b) Sauté, the onion, garlic, and crushed red pepper for 30 seconds over medium-high heat, then add the sliced calamari and all the other ingredients.

c) Bring the skillet to a boil and simmer for about three minutes, until sauce is reduced by about one-third. Serves two entrees or four appetizers.

90. Braised oxtails with red wine

Ingredient

- 6 pounds Oxtails

- 6 cups Red Wine

- $\frac{1}{2}$ cup Red Wine Vinegar

- 3 cups Cipollini Onions Or Pearl Onions

- $1\frac{1}{2}$ cup Celery, sliced

- 2 cups Carrots, sliced

- 1 teaspoon Juniper Berries
- ½ teaspoon Black Peppercorns
- Kosher Salt, Black Pepper
- ⅓cup Flour
- ¼ cup Olive Oil
- ⅓cup Tomato Paste
- 2 tablespoons Parsley

a) Place oxtails in a large nonreactive bowl. Add the wine, vinegar, cipollini onions, celery, carrots, juniper berries, peppercorns, and parsley.

b) Brown the oxtails on all sides, in oil for 10 to 15 minutes.

c) Return the oxtails to the pan with the marinade, juniper berries, peppercorns, and 2 cups water, Stir in the tomato paste until dissolved. Covered and bake for 2 hours.

d) Add the reserved vegetables. Simmer & adjust the seasoning

91. Fish in wine casserole

Ingredient

- 2 tablespoons Butter or margarine

- 1 medium Onion, thinly sliced

- $\frac{1}{2}$ cup Dry white wine

- 2 pounds Halibut fillets

- Milk

- 3 tablespoons Flour

- Salt, Pepper
- 8½ ounceCan small peas, drained
- 1½ cup Chinese fried noodles

a) Melt butter. Add onion and heat, uncovered, in Microwave Oven, 3 minutes. Add wine and fish and heat.

b) Drain pan juices into a measuring cup and add enough milk to pan juices to equal 2 cups.

c) Melt the 3 tablespoons of butter or margarine in Microwave Oven for 30 seconds.

d) Stir in flour, salt and pepper. Gradually stir in reserved fish liquid mixture.

e) Heat, uncovered, in Microwave Oven 6 minutes stirring frequently until thickened and smooth. Add peas to sauce.

f) Add sauce to fish in the casserole and stir gently. Heat, uncovered, in Microwave Oven 2 minutes. Sprinkle noodles over fish and heat. Serve

92. Wine Infused Grilled Pork Chops

Ingredient

- 2 (16 ounce) bottles Holland House® Red Cooking Wine
- 1 tablespoon chopped fresh rosemary
- 3 cloves garlic, minced
- ⅓cup packed brown sugar
- 1 ½ teaspoons table salt*
- 1 teaspoon fresh-ground pepper
- 4 (8 ounce) center cut pork chops, 3/4 inch thick

- 1 teaspoon ancho chile powder**

Directions

a) Pour cooking wine into a non-metallic container. Add sugar, salt and pepper; stir until sugar and salt are dissolved. Stir in the cooled flavor infusion.

b) Place pork chops in brine so they are completely submerged.

c) Preheat grill to medium-low heat, 325-350 degrees F.

d) Grill 10 minutes; turn and grill 4-6 minutes.

e) Remove, cover with foil and let rest 5 minutes before serving.

INFUSED DRINKS

93. Green Tea Infused Wine

INGREDIENTS:

- 8 Heaped Teaspoons of Loose Leaf Green Tea
- 1 Bottle (750ml) of Sauvignon Blanc
- Simple Syrup - Optional
- Soda Water or Lemonade - Optional

Directions:

a) Infuse the tea leaves directly in the bottle of wine, the easiest way to do this is to use a small funnel so that the leaves don't go everywhere.

b) Pop the cork back in or use a bottle stop and then place in the fridge overnight, or for a minimum of 8 hours.

c) When you are ready to drink the wine, strain out the leaves using a mesh strainer and rebottle.

d) Add simple syrup and soda or lemonade to taste - optional.

94. Refreshing wine daiquiri

Ingredient

- 1 can (6-oz) frozen lemonade

- 1 pack (10-oz) frozen strawberries; slightly thawed

- 12 ounces White wine

- Ice cubes

a) Place lemonade, strawberries and wine in blender.

b) Blend slightly. Add ice cubes and continue to blend to desired consistencyy.

95. Melon and strawberry cocktail

Ingredient

- 1 Charentals Oregon melon

- 250 grams Strawberries; washed

- 2 teaspoons Caster sugar

- 425 milliliters Dry white wine or sparkling

- 2 Sprigs mint

- 1 teaspoon Black pepper; crushed

- Orange juice

a) Cut the melon into pieces and remove seeds. Halve the strawberries and place into a bowl. Remove balls of melon using parsienne cutter and place into the bowl. sprinkle over the caster sugar, chopped mint and black pepper.

b) Pour over the orange juice and wine. Carefully stir together and refrigerate for 30 minutes to 1 hour.

c) For presentation, place the cocktail into the melon shells or into a presentation glass.

96. Jeweled wine shimmer

Ingredient

- 1 large Lemon Jello

- 1 cup Water, boiling

- 1 cup Water, cold

- 2 cups Rose wine

- $\frac{1}{2}$ cup Seedless green grapes

- $\frac{1}{2}$ cup Fresh blueberries

- 11 ounces Mandarin orange segments, drained

- Lettuce leaves

a) In large bowl, dissolve jello in boiling water; stir in cold water and wine. Chill until thickened but not set, about 1-$\frac{1}{2}$ hours. Fold in grapes, blueberries and mandarin orange segments.

b) Pour into individual molds, or an oiled 6-cup mold. Refrigerate about 4 hours or until firm. To serve, unmold on lettuce-lined serving plates.

97. Rosemary wine & black tea

Ingredient

- 1 Bottle claret; OR... other full-bodied red wine

- 1 quart Black tea pref. Assam or Darjeeling

- $\frac{1}{4}$ cup Mild honey

- ⅓cup Sugar; or to taste

- 2 Oranges sliced thin and seeded

- 2 Cinnamon sticks (3-inch)

- 6 Whole cloves

- 3 Rosemary sprigs

a) Pour the wine and tea into a noncorrodible saucepan. Add the honey, sugar, oranges, spices, and rosemary. Heat over low heat until barely steaming. Stir until the honey is dissolved.

b) Remove the pan from the heat, cover, and let stand for at least 30 minutes. When ready to serve, reheat until just steaming and serve hot

98. Earl Grey Tea Spritzer

Ingredients

- 2 tea bags of Numi Aged Earl Grey
- 1 punnet of blueberries
- A few sprigs of fresh mint
- ½ cup agave syrup
- 1 bottle sparkling white wine
- 1 tray of ice cubes

Directions

a) Bring two cups of water to boil and add the the tea bags. Let them steep for 10 minutes, adding in the agave syrup to the mix.

b) Stir a tray of ice cubes into the mixture and put it in the fridge until it cools down.

c) Once cool, add the mint and blueberries to taste, and sparkling wine, then stir together in a pitcher.

d) Enjoy!

99. Wine-Infused Hot Chocolate

INGREDIENTS

- ½ cup full cream milk
- ½ cup half-and-half – substitute with equal parts of full cream milk and light thickened cream, if unavailable
- ¼ cup/45g dark chocolate chips
- ½ cup dry red wine – preferably Shiraz
- A few drops of vanilla extract
- 1 tbsp/15ml sugar
- Tiny pinch of salt

Directions:

a) Combine the whole milk, half-and-half, dark chocolate buttons/ chips, vanilla extract and salt in a saucepan over low heat.

b) Stir constantly to prevent the chocolate at the bottom from burning, until it is fully dissolved. Once nice and hot, remove it from heat and pour in the vino. Mix well.

c) Taste the hot chocolate and adjust the sweetness using sugar. Pour into a hot chocolate mug and serve immediately.

100. Cranberry-wine punch

Ingredient

- 1½ quart Cranberry juice cocktail; chilled

- 4 cups Burgundy or other dry red wine; chilled

- 2 cups Unsweetened orange juice; chilled

- Orange slices; (optional)

a) Combine first 3 ingredients in a large bowl; stir well.

b) Garnish with orange slices, if desired.

CONCLUSION

Modern recipe makers spend much time touting homemade infusions, tinctures and wine-infused dishes. And for good reason: Custom syrups and liqueurs allow bars to create signature cocktails that can't always be replicated. For bar managers and owners looking to make the most of thin operating margins, it's cheaper to make something "bespoke" with leftover ingredients from a restaurant's kitchen, than paying for premade commercial offerings.

Most ingredients can be used to infuse with wine. However, ingredients that have natural water content in them, like fresh fruits, tend to perform better.

However, the choice is yours, and experimentation is part of the fun. Whichever you try, the results will be enjoyable!

Lightning Source UK Ltd.
Milton Keynes UK
UKHW020712311221
396434UK00005B/33